Autism Supporting Difficulties

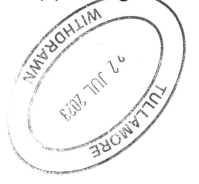

The cover image is a painting by myself which was inspired by the Ancient Greek concept of nous relating to our inner selves. The image was inspired by the Greek symbols/ and intends to represent the depths of knowledge and understanding children and adults with autism spectrum conditions have within them yet we find it hard to access each other's inner selves.

Autism
Supporting
Difficulties

Handbook of ideas to reduce anxiety
in everyday situations

Gaynor Jackson

Matador
9 Priory Business Park,
Wistow Road, Kibworth Beauchamp,
Leicestershire. LE8 0RX
Tel: 0116 279 2299
Email: books@troubador.co.uk
Web: www.troubador.co.uk/matador
Twitter: @matadorbooks

ISBN 978 1785893 872

British Library Cataloguing in Publication Data.
A catalogue record for this book is available from the British Library.

Typeset in 11pt Minion Pro by Troubador Publishing Ltd, Leicester, UK

Matador is an imprint of Troubador Publishing Ltd

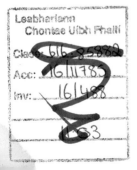

Acknowledgements

*All of the amazing parents and children who have inspired
me by their determination and success.*

TABLE OF CONTENTS

INTRODUCTION

The aim of this book is to provide ideas and guidelines that will help parents, educators, and children with autism spectrum disorder (ASD) themselves, learn to manage their difficulties.

I have worked in inclusive mainstream schools and as an advisory teacher working with young children with social communication difficulties and a range of special needs. My most formative time has been working in resourced provisions for children with autism spectrum disorders (ASD), and during the course of my studies which specialised in children with ASD and their needs. I have worked with numerous parents of children with ASD in the course of my career and students who have been inspirational in their patience and perseverance. Over the years I have found that there are many common difficulties, especially for parents of children who have been recently diagnosed. Some of these parents may wait in excess of twelve months to attend courses to inform and support them. To their credit many independently search the Internet for solutions, interventions and strategies which they can adopt to support their children's needs. Some of the parents with whom I have worked have found claims of 'cures' by some on these websites which has tempted them to try some more unusual and unproven 'remedies', despite the fact that ASD is a lifelong difficulty as described by the National Autistic Society:

'Autism is a lifelong developmental disability that affects how a person communicates with, and relates to, other people. It also affects how they make sense of the world around them.' (National Autistic Society, 2014)

Consequently, I wanted to write this short book to provide some ideas and re-enforcement as to how common some of these difficulties are, and provide some simple and I hope informative tips about how children with ASD can be supported by their parents and professionals to take steps to manage their anxieties and difficulties. From my work and studies with parents and professionals I have selected a range of strategies and interventions which I have used to help children with ASD try to overcome the daily difficulties that they encounter and in most of these cases have helped them learn to manage these difficulties more effectively.

Children with ASD often have difficulty processing information; they generally have a liking for sameness and routine, and have hyper (over) and hypo (under) sensitivities (Bogdashina, 2003). The combination of these difficulties for children with ASD often cause anxiety and tantrums to come to the surface. Unfortunately there is no one standard solution for any of the difficulties experienced; however, the suggestions offered here should help parents and carers of children with ASD and school staff to enable their children to tolerate contexts or objects which cause them anxiety and distress.

I would like to commend the parents whom I have worked with for their energy and patience.

I have included vignettes in the text to illustrate some of the difficulties encountered and the effect of using certain interventions. The names of any children whose behaviours and difficulties I have worked with and used in my text have been changed to ensure their anonymity.

We should always remember that children are individuals no matter what difficulties they have in common. Autism is a Spectrum of Difficulties and is now known to incorporate elements of sensory sensitivities that impact heavily on the daily lives of those affected. Children's degrees of difficulties and sensory issues are not uniform but are individual to each child. However, they may be improved by the same or very similar interventions once the underlying causes or triggers have been identified.

Chapter One
BOOKS –
CREATING INTEREST

Children with ASD may enjoy books about their special interests.

Many children (not just those with ASD) are not interested in books; however, if you take photos of the children doing various activities and make these into a book about themselves they often become interested and an enjoyment of books starts to develop.

If your child likes using cameras or iPads they may enjoy taking photos of themselves or of things that they like. You can then help them make these pictures into a book, adding some text (even if they can't yet read); they may like to hear you read the text to them and, who knows, in time they may learn to read themselves.

Some children with autism are hyperlexic (they are able to read from a very early age) however, this does not mean that they understand what they are reading. You can assess this by asking them questions about what they have read, for example What did x do? What was the x's name? Where did x go?

Children with autism may read or listen to a story but have difficulty processing information. This may make questions about what has happened extremely difficult to answer. However, it may help them to answer some simple questions if they are shown the relevant pages of the book.

Suggestions of subjects could include:

- Trips
- Family members
- The children themselves and their favourite cartoon characters
- Play areas in school or at home where a picture of your child can slide between the pages
- Social stories (Gray and White, 2002) designed to help young children learn life skills and social skills
- Anything your child likes to cut out and stick, for example, pictures and coloured or textured paper
- Books about activities that your child enjoys or that include their own drawings

These can be extended to include opportunities for matching pictures or adding missing words, for example, using a picture of your child digging with a grey spade:

X has a   Spade

Each of the coloured squares will need Velcro on the reverse so that they can be selected and attached to the space on the page.

Ask your child to choose which colour matches the picture from two or three options e.g. black, white or grey, then attach it to the sentence. Praise your child's efforts and if they make a mistake say something encouraging like 'good try', pause, then 'try again' (I would remove the incorrect colour if you are using three choices as this will make the task easier).

X has a   grey   spade
           (With child's
           choice attached)

Martin

I first worked with Martin when he was in nursery; he didn't like books at all. He wouldn't even look at a book, let alone choose one to take home in his book bag. To try to gain his interest I took photos of him at various activities which he enjoyed and made them into a book. I included some simple text and some spaces where missing words could be attached. The missing words were accompanied by pictures on small squares the same size as the spaces. He wasn't able to read the words but with the images next to them he could understand what they meant. These had Velcro on the back so that the correct image/word could be selected and stuck into the space in the text. The first time he saw the book he was vaguely interested for a few seconds. The second time he wanted to look at the photos of himself, which gradually increased to him looking at all of the photos on all of the pages. He then watched me model how to find the missing word (from a selection attached to the last page of the book) and put it into the sentence. After a few sessions he couldn't wait to come and see the book and attach the missing words/pictures; in fact, he would often request it if we asked him to choose an activity. He liked the book so much that we made another including pictures of him and his favourite cartoon characters. He subsequently started to want to choose and take home reading books from school and sometimes he even chose independently to sit and look at books in the quiet corner.

Books can often be a great resource to help children choose and match.

Try taking a picture of your child and some pages of their favoured toys, add Velcro to both so that the image of your child can be attached. Ask your child to attach the photo of themselves to the page representing the toy that they want to play with – simply say "choose" and show the pages. Help them to select a toy if they are unable to do so independently (they will gain confidence and understand with practice, although this may take some time). Once they have chosen the toy, take them to it to play.

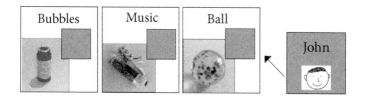

Hussain

Hussain was not able to choose which activity he wanted at the nursery and he found it very difficult to move between activities without becoming anxious and screaming for extended periods, at which time he was inconsolable. Hussain could say some simple words and phrases although he was very difficult to understand, so often got frustrated, which again led to an outburst of screaming. At one time the other children in the class put their hands over their ears as they didn't like the high-pitched noise.

I made Hussain a book of photographs of different areas of the class, showing which activity would be there, e.g. the home corner, painting table, sand table, puzzle corner. I then took a photograph of Hussain and made some slits in each of the photo pages so that the photo of him could be inserted through the page and he would appear in the scene, e.g. Hussain would be at the painting table. We started to use the book with Hussain to show him the activities and tried to encourage him to choose a page; we then showed him how to slide his picture into the scene, at which point we would walk to the chosen activity together and use the equipment that we found. To our great pleasure he joined in with us. Hussain loved this book; he often looked for it and clearly understood that he could use it to choose what he wanted to do which helped him become more independent and confident to move between activities. His screaming didn't disappear altogether but it was noticeably reduced. Sometimes he just wanted to slide his picture through all of the pages before he chose; it became a popular and important activity for him.

With the help of this book Hussain was able to communicate to us which activity he wanted to access, and we were able to use it to move him on from equipment which he would have previously refused to leave.

An example of one or two of the pages:

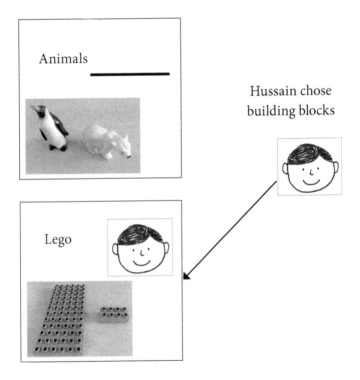

Animals

Hussain chose
building blocks

Lego

Chapter Two
BOTTLES AND CUPS – GENERALISING SKILLS

Children with ASD find it difficult to generalise skills. They like routine and may only drink from one type/colour of bottle or cup, or only drink in one place, e.g. home, not school.

It may not seem like a big issue but if they stop manufacturing the particular cup, your child may refuse to drink. In order to avoid this you may find it easier to use a range of cups or bottles, as well as encouraging your child to drink in different places in the house and at school.

If your child finds it difficult to make the transition from bottle to cup you could try one of the following suggestions:

- Take them to the shop to choose the cup.
- Ask a sibling to show them how to drink from the cup.
- Pour most of the drink into the cup from the bottle so that they see the drink in the bottle (which they are familiar with), have a small drink from the bottle, but if they want more, they are offered the cup.
- Choose a cup with a picture of their favourite cartoon character on it.

Changes to beaker or cup from a bottle may take a long time; make sure you praise your child even if they only get the cup to their lips for the first few attempts. Always try to finish on a good note as this is what they will remember.

If they spill the drink don't make a fuss as this may put them off next time.

Your child may have a preference for certain types of cups based on:

- Material – rigid or soft plastic, thick or thin pottery
- Colour
- Size
- Shape
- Handle – shape and grip

If your child has a preference for a particular colour it is a good idea to let the school know. If the school can use the same colour your child is more likely to drink, whereas if school offers an alternative colour your child may refuse to use it, as they may not be able to generalise that this is in fact a cup. Alternatively, you may be able to supply the school with a familiar cup from home.

These are all things which may impact on your child's acceptance of new cups, etc. Whenever you can, take this into account when purchasing or introducing new drinking vessels.

Try to note which cups they will use in order to decide on new ones. It is too late when the old one becomes worn out, broken or lost if it is no longer being manufactured and your child has only ever used the one type.

Janet

Janet enjoyed drinking from a bottle and was very particular about having the same teat. The manufacturers stopped making this particular teat and Janet's mother had a very difficult job getting Janet to drink. Her mother was extremely worried; she tried using a syringe to squirt small amounts of water into Janet's mouth as she refused the bottle with the different teat. Fortunately, Janet was eventually coaxed to drink from a beaker with her favourite cartoon character on it.

Chapter Three
CHOICES – ENCOURAGING COMMUNICATION

As parents, we often pre-empt what our children want whether they have special needs or not, for example:

Bic = biscuit

Dink = drink

Pointing – the adult guesses and offers objects one at a time by lifting them up and naming them. If we want our child to communicate more clearly we need to encourage them, for example:

- If they want a drink, show them two options (objects), e.g. milk in one hand and juice in the other.
- When they choose by reaching for one, name it, e.g. "Oh, John wants juice" and offer the juice.

Repeat this whenever they want something even if you know what it is – it will encourage them to develop a clearer form of communication.

If they use Picture Exchange Communication System (Frost and Bondy, 2002), they will specify choice by using symbols. If they are at the stage where they can discriminate, make sure there are several choices in their PECS book.

If they speak they may reach and name the object

themselves; however, if they just reach we can help them become familiar with the object by naming it.

This strategy can be used with toys, clothes and activities and is a useful one to remember.

It is worth considering that although as parents we know what our children want almost instinctively, it doesn't help them learn to communicate. There may be times when we aren't available, for example, at school or if we have an emergency, so it's really important that we teach them how to communicate and make choices whether it be verbally, using symbols or pictures, pointing or leading us by the hand.

If our children aren't able to make us understand what they want, they may become extremely distressed or upset and may hit out or run, so if we can help them develop an effective means of communicating choices it will help them for life.

Chapter Four
CLOTHES – ACCEPTING NEW CLOTHES

How exciting to most children to have new clothes, but to a child with ASD it can be very upsetting.

Why?
Sensory sensitivities – fabric, colour, smell, likeness for the familiar. It may not necessarily relate to stubbornness and may therefore take some time to overcome but this will be worth it in the long term.

Fabric – encourage your child to feel the clothes in the shop before you buy them if you can. Give them to your child to explore before you try to get your child to wear them. If they are wary of touching them, keep placing them near or touching a favourite toy so that your child has to touch them to get to the toy (e.g. put them on their teddy, or drape them over a favourite toy car); keep doing this until they are happy to touch them and explore them.

Try getting your child to wear them even if it's for a few minutes – you can gradually extend this – and you could also use 'now and next', e.g. new clothes on next favourite toy, e.g. bear.

Now	Next
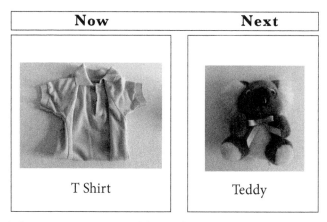	
T Shirt	Teddy

Colour – some parents like to dress their children in the same colour, although personally I think it is better to change colours to help your child tolerate change more easily (unless you have a more important reason for making that choice).

Stuart

I knew some parents who preferred to dress their son in an orange T shirt whenever they could. The reason for this was that he was a runner and it was much easier to see him if he ran off. By dressing him in orange this immediately helped to reduce the number of children who they needed to look at to find him. Orange tee shirts thereby saved the parents' time and a certain amount of worry. His parents had observed that there were never many children wearing orange and this strategy was highly successful in helping them if he ran off, for example, in the park where there was a large group of children.

Smell – wash new clothes before attempting to get your child to wear them as then they will smell more familiar.

Routine/liking for sameness – Try to vary types of clothes from an early age; of course, it is possible to buy the same style in a range of sizes but at some stage your child may outgrow the style or size, or the item may cease being manufactured, so it may only provide a short-term answer.

Make slight changes, e.g. same colour or pattern but different style, or same style but different colour.

You could cut a little patch from clothes being replaced and let your child keep this in the pocket of new trousers or sew the patch on the new clothes; if it's a really difficult problem to discard the old item completely, children may find this reassuring.

Chapter Five
COMPUTERS AND IPADS –
THE NEED FOR MODERATION

This seems completely at odds with this book as there are very few parents I have heard complain about the time that their children spend using computers or iPads.

Computers, iPads and interactive technology are indisputably the way ahead, but my question would be: do they teach social skills?

Often children with ASD have an amazing understanding of computer programs and are able to operate these way beyond their developmental years; however, whilst this is certainly an achievement it doesn't help them make friends, or learn to interact with others, so their advantages are limited, and consequently so should the time children spend using them.

Some children are exceedingly keen and able in using computer programs but so fixated on them that they may demand to dress themselves or eat their supper in front of them. I do understand that this enables them to sit still or focus, similar to sitting them in front of the TV, but in respect of life skills, negotiation and socialising it may be lacking.

We generally all like to spend time alone relaxing,

reading a book, etc. but we also need the skills to negotiate in order to ask for what we want, do our shopping or find our way if we are lost.

Computers and iPads are wonderful pieces of technology but we need to control the amount of time children spend on these in order to ensure that other skills develop, unless of course children are using them to support their communication with apps and programs that provide a range of picture symbols or speech generating devices.

Joe

One of the parents I worked with spoke to me about her son Joe and how he wouldn't let his two brothers watch what they wanted on TV or use the programs that they wanted on the iPad. I suggested she use a traffic light system for everyone in the household, e.g. each person had a name tag with their photograph included (as Joe couldn't yet read): if it was Joe's time on the computer his name and photograph would be on green; if Joe was waiting it would be on orange; and if Joe had had a turn or did not want a turn his name would be on red; gradually moving between the traffic lights. Amazingly, it worked straight away and Joe didn't even attempt to argue about what program was showing when it wasn't his turn. So in some ways maybe computers and iPads can teach some social skills related to sharing and taking turns.

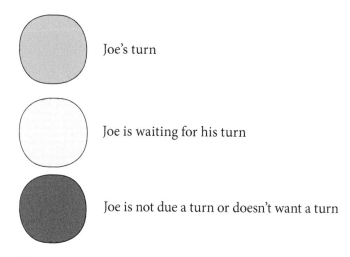

Joe's turn

Joe is waiting for his turn

Joe is not due a turn or doesn't want a turn

There are many useful programs on iPads and computers for children with ASD, including those related to toilet training and picture communication. They can be used to show the sequence of events or to learn new skills and to entertain children when they are likely to become anxious. Children also generally like watching footage of themselves and their families. Computers and iPads are extremely useful as long as they are used with some element of parental control.

Remember who is in charge and don't let your child dictate which programs you access and for how long, as this can escalate to other scenarios very quickly.

Chapter Six
DENTISTS –
REDUCING THE FEAR

Quite a frightening experience for many of us! … because it may hurt and it's always different each time you visit, so no wonder it's difficult for a child with ASD.

- Dentists' surgeries are not routine places we visit:
- Smell – they smell of mouthwash, especially to a child with a hypersensitive sense of smell.
- Sound – they do sound a bit scary sometimes as you can hear the drill, but even more scary are the sounds of patients moaning or crying.
- Visually – they have bright lights on moving arms.
- Unfamiliar – they aren't like anywhere else you visit; they have chairs that go up and down, whizzy mouthwash sinks and the people who work there wear masks. They expect us to sit with our mouths wide open and not make noises or eat with them. The dentists put things in our mouths which we aren't allowed to eat, e.g. metal objects.

Some ideas about how we can reduce children with ASD's fears and anxieties about visiting dentists:

- Use or smell mouthwash regularly at home.
- Practise looking in each other's mouths and touching each other's teeth.
- Listen to drill sounds and play with toys which vibrate and hum.
- Look at photos of dentists' surgeries and equipment and, if your child is verbal, talk about what the things do. If you can take or obtain photos of the actual dentist's surgery you visit and the staff, look at these with your child and prepare them for the visit.
- Talk to your dentist and explain that your child has ASD and that they may be very anxious about the visit.
- If you think your child may sit in the chair, let them watch it going up and down, perhaps with you on it having your teeth inspected first. If you think this is going to be too scary for your child it may be best avoided; ask if your child could sit on either an ordinary chair or on your lap.
- Try to visit the dentist regularly; the more often you go the less anxious your child will be.

If you ask the receptionist they will generally be happy for you and your child to visit and sit in the waiting room for a few minutes even if you don't have an appointment. This will help your child become familiar with the environment. You could make this an even more enjoyable experience by giving your child something nice to play with while they are there, e.g. a favourite comic, car or even a particular food, although this would probably be best given after they come out as if you do go for a check-up it is easier if your child doesn't have a mouthful of food.

Now	**Next**
Dentist	Park

You could use 'now and next', e.g. now dentist, next Park.
Or a sequence of pictures.

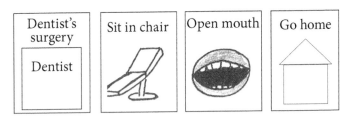

Dentist's surgery	Sit in chair	Open mouth	Go home
Dentist			

Persevere because if your child does get toothache it is much better if it isn't the first visit and they are used to the dental surgery. I don't know of anyone who has avoided the dentist for life; the more often you go the more familiar and less scary it becomes, not just for children with ASD but for us all.

Chapter Seven
DOCTORS AND HOSPITALS – MAKING IT A PLEASANT EXPERIENCE

Children with ASD have remarkable memories and it is consequently highly likely that their first memory of visiting the doctor may relate to vaccinations or injections that would have been a very unpleasant experience.

As with all unfamiliar trips it is essential to prepare your child for the visit. You can do this by looking at books about the doctors, pictures of the surgery and any instruments that he may use, for example, stethoscopes online before you go. It may be worth buying a toy doctor's kit which you can pretend to use on each other.

Your child may be reassured by using 'now and next' or by a tempting reward, e.g. a toy or snack.

(If they don't understand pictures show them the crisps, but don't give them all to your child before the doctor examines them or there will be no reward to give.)

Now	Next
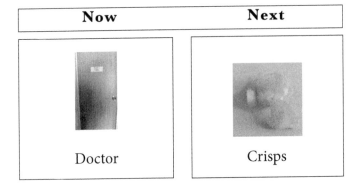	
Doctor	Crisps

It may be worth visiting the doctor's surgery just to look inside if you are passing. Explain to the surgery that your child is anxious about visits due to having ASD, and they should be quite happy for you to sit in the waiting room and explore the toys for five minutes now and again.

If the doctor wants to use a stethoscope or some other unfamiliar equipment, ask the doctor if your child can explore it first; perhaps you could ask the receptionist if you could have an extended appointment so that you don't have to rush and your child has time to accept the context and this new person who wants to look at them, their ears or wherever the problem is.

If your child is really upset by the thought and experience of going into the surgery and waiting with everyone else, ask if you can have an early or late appointment as the waiting room will be less busy, and explain why. Often, people are very obliging if you ask them to help, but they don't always know instinctively what to do unless you make suggestions.

Hospitals may be even more daunting, especially if your child has to stay in; I would recommend that you make a book about hospitals together or borrow a book from the library to look at together. If your child understands verbal description explain to them what it will be like, what will happen and that they will come home in x number of days.

If they find it difficult to understand and process words, use pictures similar to that shown in the dentist chapter 6 to make a sequence about what will happen, but remember to put home at the end so that your child is reassured that they will come home afterwards.

Chapter Eight
FOOD AND DRINK – EXTENDING RESTRICTED EATING

It is not only children with ASD who are picky eaters or have a restricted diet; many children find it hard to tolerate different foods. However, for the child with ASD, sensory issues may have a great impact – smell, taste, visual appearance and texture can impact significantly on their eating habits. Context and changes of location may also impact on your child's eating habits.

Trial and error is the only way to determine which foods your child will eat, but it may be a good idea to start with a basic, plain, bland base first.

Give them a selection of basic foods and see which they choose, for example:

- Pasta – different shapes, plain or with various sauces
- Rice – brown, white, long grain, short grain, with vegetables
- Bread – soft, crusty, toast, brown, white, round, square (you could help your child choose and cut the shape using cake cutters)

- Potatoes – boiled, mashed, roasted, chips, croquettes
- Vegetables – white (parsnip, cauliflower), green (broccoli, cabbage, peas, beans), orange (carrots, sweet potato), yellow (corn, peppers, courgettes), purple (aubergine, beetroot)

Provide opportunities for your child to play with food, for example:

- A variety of dips with finger foods to try, or spoons dipped in different foodstuffs
- Build towers with slices of carrot
- Make lines of cubed foods or breadsticks and dry spaghetti
- Put small pieces of food on toy cars, trucks or trains as you play with them

It may be that your child will only eat dry food. If this is the case, make a variety of mashed vegetables coated in breadcrumbs and fried in patties.

If it is wet food that your child likes, you may find that having a selection of sauces available with each meal to dip into helps them to try slightly dryer foods.

Try to analyse what your child does eat and find a similar food to try in addition; it is important that children have a balanced diet and if you are struggling ask your GP to refer you to a nutritionist who may be able to give you support and some new ideas.

Many children whom I have worked with drink a lot of milk for their age which makes them feel full; however, as they grow they need nourishment from additional food in order to grow and remain healthy. They may like the sensation of drinking in which case, if they find it hard to eat solid food, you could try smoothies or soups from a cup. It is difficult for your child to eat if they are full of milk, so it may be more beneficial to offer this after they have eaten a sufficient amount, but beware that some children, not just those with ASD, will wait for the milk and rather refuse food. If you are nervous about adjusting your child's diet and believe that they will refuse food, seek advice from your doctor or clinic who may be able to refer you to a nutritionist or occupational therapist (dependent upon the cause of their restricted diet) before you make any changes to their food.

Stevie and Cheryl

Stevie and Cheryl were both poor eaters, especially at school. I started some simple cookery sessions with them. Initially I had two fruits – a banana and an apple – from which they could choose by reaching as I held them both out. The aim was to make sandwiches; however, Cheryl ate the bread whilst Stevie really enjoyed cutting the banana and by chance licked his fingers. It seemed like a positive start.

I brought in cooked pasta for the children to explore and make letters with on the table one day; they both ate some, in fact Stevie couldn't get enough – he kept eating it.

The most memorable cooking activity was when we made pizza; by this time the children were able to identify the ingredients by matching them to pictures, and with some adult support follow a visual structure of how to make the dough. Stevie and Cheryl loved rolling the dough base and spooning on the tomato. They were even able to choose their toppings from sweetcorn or pepper and mushrooms or peas and add these (although some were eaten before they touched the pizza base). The pizzas were taken away to be cooked and when they came back Cheryl had a bite of hers, and Stevie, after giving his a good smell, licked off the topping. Both the staff and the parents celebrated what we all recognised as a great achievement which could be gradually built on and extended.

Chapter Nine
FRIENDS AND FRIENDSHIPS –
SOCIAL CONFIDENCE

Social interaction is a source of anxiety for children with ASD. Children with ASD often don't understand what is appropriate and what is not, which can result in them tugging their peers' collars or pushing them to gain their attention. They may only want to play, but this behaviour often alienates their peers so it's important to try to help build their confidence and ability to approach others in an appropriate way.

Ask one of your friend's children or one of the children at school to your house to play. Talk to the other child's mother to explain that your child has ASD and that it's difficult for them to make friends so you would like to help them. Explain any special interests your child may have, how they communicate (if it's not verbally) if you feel this information will help people understand how they behave.

Sit with them and help them share an activity, e.g. building a tower and knocking it down or sharing a jigsaw puzzle. Repeat this several times.

Maybe they could share some food that they both like; if your child has a limited diet they could just sit together. It may encourage your child to try something new.

Repeat these suggestions several times before extending the activity. If your child accepts this you could try asking different children.

Be cautious about invitations back to the friends' houses as they may not be quite as easy. At home in contrast your child knows the routine, the context and is in familiar surroundings which may help them cope with the introduction of a friend. If they are invited back to a friend's house it may be best if you go with them the first couple of times, and I would explain this to the other child's parents before the event.

If you decide to go to the friend's house and feel that your child can cope with this, either with you or on their own, these are some useful tips:

- Ask the friend for a photo of their house and anyone else who will be there, e.g. siblings or pets.
- Look at the photos and talk about what is going to happen on the visit with your child.
- Make the visit short the first time; it may be wise not to eat at the friend's house as this may be too stressful for your child.
- It may be best if you stay with them or at least relatively close to them in case there is a problem.
- Try to end the visit while your child is happy. If it ends when they are distressed this is probably what they will remember and the next visit may prove extremely difficult, so it may be better to leave early whilst they are still enjoying themselves.

It may often seem that children with ASD prefer to play with older children; this may be because they are more predictable. Younger children are still learning about negotiating and sharing and can be unpredictable. This can present a significant cause for anxiety in children with ASD as they are unsure what response they will receive from young children; they may take their favourite toys or push and hit without warning as they are themselves still learning to negotiate. However, it is worth persevering with peers as it may help your child to make more friends at school, who in turn will be there to help and support your child in the future, and in the community.

Chapter Ten
HAIRCUTS AND HAIR CARE –
FAMILIARISING YOUR CHILD

So many parents tell a similar story about how their children become very anxious when faced with a trip to the hairdresser. It seems unfair that long hair even today seems more widely accepted for girls than boys, resulting in parents feeling additional pressure to keep their boys' hair short. Many parents resort to holding their children whilst barbers hurriedly use clippers to complete the deed. Mothers who have never cut hair before find it becomes their job to snip the long hair to a more acceptable length as best they can.

The best way to avoid your child becoming anxious is to try to familiarise your child with the experience at an early age.

As soon as any anxiety becomes apparent, many parents tend to avoid or delay cutting their children's hair, but it doesn't make it easier – it makes the anxiety worse as there are fewer trips.

Before you can find the solution you need to identify the cause:

1. Clippers – the sound or feel of the vibrating blades against the head or hair

2. Combs – the sound of combing, sensation of pulling the hair, scratching the scalp, coldness of metal combs
3. Hairdryers – the sound in the background as well as those being used on the children, the heat in the atmosphere
4. Hairspray – the smell and sound of spraying
5. Shop – small space, number of people in close proximity
6. Scissors – the sound of cutting, touch of scissors on hair, some young people with ASD who are more able to communicate report it physically hurts when their hair is cut.

Some strategies that may help to overcome specific fears and anxieties:

1. Clippers

Encourage your child to listen to the clippers from a distance, gradually bringing them nearer as their anxiety lessens (this may take weeks or months).

Carefully place the back of the clippers against your child's fingers (opposite blade side) so that they can feel the vibration, initially for a couple of seconds gradually building up (take your time as above).

Start to move the back of the clipper back over hands just for a few seconds, increasing the time as your child becomes less anxious.

Try moving the back of the clipper back up arms, working up towards the neck and finally onto the head (don't rush these steps).

Clip a very small section of hair, very gradually building up to the complete haircut; again, this cannot be rushed.

2. Combs

Comb your hair with the back of a comb and encourage your child to help you; comb your child's hair with the back of the comb (take turns doing it to each other).

Turn the comb and pass it once through a section of untangled hair and repeat this until your child's anxiety has passed and then try two comb motions (take turns if this reassures your child), gradually increasing but always stopping whilst your child is happy.

You could also encourage your child to comb dolls' hair.

3. Hairdryers

Let your child handle a dryer which is unplugged until they can accept it. Plug it in and repeat the above. Turn it on briefly (a few seconds), turning it off before your child becomes anxious. Gradually increase the time it is on. Use it to blow paper or feathers as a game and occasionally briefly let the air blow on your child's hair (seconds only to begin with). Increase the time the hairdryer is on. Encourage your child to help you dry your hair. Dry a small section of their hair, gradually increasing to their whole head.

Alternatively

Speak to the hairdresser and arrange to visit when it's quiet and ask them not to use dryers while you are there (you may be surprised how understanding some hairdressers are).

4. Hairspray

Explain to the hairdresser that this makes your child anxious and frightened; ask them not to use it whilst you are in the shop, or arrange your visit at a quiet time. Let your child smell the can and hold it; if possible, have two types which they can choose from as they may like one smell better. Spray the can very briefly, some distance away from your child; if your child isn't anxious, gradually move towards them and repeat brief spraying. Expose your child to very small amounts of water spray first, gradually building up to hairspray and then increase the amount.

5. Hairdressing premises

Go to the shop often, just to walk in and walk out. When this is acceptable to your child, start to say hello to the hairdresser. Sit in the waiting area and give your child a favourite snack or a toy to play with for a few minutes, then go home. Go to the shop, let your child sit in a barber's chair and eat the snack or play with the toy. If the chairs go up and down, your child may need time to watch this happening before and if they are able to experience it themselves. Go to the shop, let your child sit in the barber's chair and show your child the snack or toy and explain that it is the haircut first then the snack. If your child will only tolerate one snip of hair, stop here; if they are not anxious, cut more hair but always try to stop before they become anxious, and give the snack. Gradually work towards a whole head of hair being cut but continue regular 'pleasant' visits with no cutting involved in between, just to keep familiar with the context.

6. Scissors

Encourage your child to listen to the scissors as you snip in the air from a distance, gradually bringing them nearer as their anxiety lessens (this may take weeks or months). Place the scissors near your child's head and snip the air around them, initially for a couple of seconds, gradually building up as above. Cut a very small section of hair, very gradually building up to the complete haircut.

Chapter Eleven
HAIR WASHING – MAKING IT PAIN FREE

The sensory aspect: some adults with ASD report that it feels like needles dropping on them when they stand under a shower, which must surely also affect how they feel during hair washing too!

In addition to this it hurts most people when the shampoo gets in their eyes, if their head is rubbed too hard or the water is too hot or too cold.

As a child I used to beg my mother not to dry my hair as she always included rubbing my ears which really hurt!

Some suggestions:
- Make it fun.
- Use 'now and next' with visuals, e.g. now hair wash, next TV.
- Use mild shampoos.

Avoiding washing hair isn't the answer as it will escalate into a major problem; suppose your child gets food or paint in their hair or even worse becomes infected with nits.

Some chemists stock a type of collar for the head to stop shampoo going in a child's eyes – this may help.

Try washing their hair whilst they are in the bath by getting them to lie backwards in the water and maybe hold a flannel over their eyes.

In extreme cases of anxiety you could try using a dry shampoo in between washes on the agreement that every third wash is with water, or alternatively, if they refuse the dry hair wash, it's going to be more often.

Take your child to the shops, let them smell the shampoos and choose one they like the smell of –baby shampoos are usually gentler and sting less.

Start by washing a dolly's hair together, then maybe try just washing the tips of their hair, followed of course by something nice – a special drink or biscuit and a cuddle together. You can build on this bit by bit. Wash the back of their hair and gradually work towards the front, maybe just using the tiniest bit of shampoo at the front or even just water to begin with.

You could also let your child watch any siblings and yourself wash hair to see what happens as a bystander.

I have seen a DVD called "I can wash my hair" (I Can Kids Ltd, 2010) that models washing hair and has some positive reviews. The activity is accompanied by singing and routine actions; if your child likes music they may enjoy using this. Alternatively, you could make up your own song to a known tune, for example, 'Here We Go Round the Mulberry Bush' – 'This is the way we wash our hair'.

Chapter Twelve
HOLIDAYS –
PREPARING FOR SUCCESS

Preparation and Planning

Holidays need a lot of preparation for everyone – it is the most important key to a successful holiday. Finding the right holiday package – venue, dates, mode of travel, what to take – is stressful for anyone. If you also have the needs of a child with ASD to take into account, in order to make it a successful trip for all the family it can be extremely complicated. For a child with ASD who has a liking for routine what could be scarier? In order to alleviate some of this anxiety you can:

- Look at possible holidays together.
- Think about the best way to travel – if your child loves trains why not incorporate one in the journey or a trip whilst you are away.
- Try to get a brochure if it's available and look at it every day before you go. Start this as early as you can. If no brochure is available make your own with pictures from the Internet or photos.
- Take pictures of their favourite toys and superimpose

them onto pictures of where you are going to reassure them that you will take these with you.

- Make a list of words or pictures about things you are going to do whilst you are on holiday and look at it regularly.
- Make a scrapbook about where you are going (which could include the above) and how you will get there. Include photos of the venue and surroundings. Most importantly of all, have a picture of you all coming home at the end.

Advise the holiday rep, venue, or travel company that your child has special needs and may become upset at some time during the holiday; they will often make allowances or concessions in this event, for example:

- Boarding early on planes or sitting next to empty seats if there are any.
- Adjusting the location of your room, caravan, etc. to a quieter area, park, or space, etc. if it will be of benefit to you.
- Preferential queuing.
- Catering for special diets.

When travelling, take your child's favourite toy and/or food to reassure them. If they are young take their familiar potty, plate, spoon, cup and any favourite objects that you think they will miss and become anxious for.

Look at your scrapbook every day before you go. It will help your child to know what to expect.

On Holiday

New surroundings can cause anxiety; children with ASD don't always understand that holidays are short-term and may think they will never go home. This can be reinforced with visuals – a picture of the holiday home and a picture of home in sequence, for example:

Now	Next
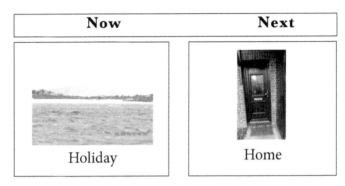 Holiday	Home

Children may become anxious if they are surrounded by different smells, objects and noises.

Use some familiar things, e.g. your child's duvet cover which will look and smell familiar and/or a favourite toy, beaker or treat to help alleviate this.

If your child is a runner you may want to make them more visible by always dressing them in a coloured T-shirt. This will reduce the number of people you need to look at to locate them if they do run.

Some parents like to carry cards which advise that their child has ASD and that this may affect their behaviour; it's a simple way of informing people without the necessity of a long drawn-out conversation.

If you need something, ask the holiday rep, proprietor

or tour operator. Most holiday establishments are keen to help – after all, you are paying them.

Whilst you are on holiday take photos, pictures and make films; even if your child is pre-verbal they can still share these things and memories with you when you get home. Collect any small items your child finds interesting to add to the holiday items, for example, sea shells, ice-cream wrappers, a small pot of sand, and bring them back so that you can all reminisce about your holiday. You could make a collage or a book with them together when you get home. If your child is at school they will be able to take these things to show and share with their peers and teachers when they return to school.

Most important of all, enjoy your holiday.

Chapter Thirteen
PACKED LUNCHES OR SCHOOL DINNERS – LEARNING TO EAT A PACKED LUNCH

This is a major decision in itself, especially if your child has a limited diet for one reason or another. Many children with or without ASD have limited diets, sometimes due to taste, texture or maybe just preference for the sweet or savoury foods, but whatever the reason, it will need addressing as otherwise it can cause them to have a more and more restricted diet which could impact on their health, mood and well-being.

If you intend to give your child a packed lunch you will need to give them something they like. It will be difficult for them to eat a sandwich if they have never had one before. They will need to become familiar with eating from a packed lunch bag or box – if they always eat off a plate they may not know what to do with a packed lunch bag. If they always drink from a beaker they may not know how to drink from a carton with a straw. You will need to do some preparation at home in the summer holidays before they start staying for lunch. It may help to borrow a school dinner tray for the holidays and teach them to eat savoury from one section and sweet from another with a cup in situ. This is quite different to the arrangements we have at home with a separate plate and dish, so the more you can practise the better.

If your child is used to following a visual structure they may benefit from a visual list of lunch items which you could draw or photograph, for example:

| Sandwich | Drink | Jelly | Cake |

The menu for school dinners should be available from the school office, so maybe you can try some of the things in the holidays or maybe you only want your child to stay when you know they will like the food, e.g. fish fingers and chips or pasta and salad.

The children may take their cue from their peers who could help and encourage them to try more food and drink, but it may not always have an impact.

Many children with ASD find the dinner hall a terrifying place – it is loud, smelly, bright and full of moving bodies.

Speak to the school about your child and the potential difficulties they may experience in the dinner hall. Some schools will make arrangements for your child to be given their lunch in a quieter area or go on to the dining hall slightly earlier than the other children when there are less children and it is less daunting. Be prepared – even with these strategies it may take some time for your child to eat at school. Many of the children I have worked with won't eat anything to begin with but with patience and the use of visuals and encouragement, they do eventually make progress.

Chapter Fourteen
PARTIES –
GETTING BEYOND THE
ENTRANCE

How exciting to receive an invite to a party... or is it? For a child with ASD or their family this can be a situation of dread. Children with ASD generally like the familiar and often become anxious when faced with the unknown. Many children with ASD lack imagination. The prospect of a party can therefore create a feeling of anxiety for various reasons. What's behind the large heavy doors of a church hall? Why are children screaming behind the walls and doors of this unfamiliar building? Will it be smelly, bright, noisy or crowded inside? Will children or adults touch the things I want?

Careful preparation may help

Visit the venue before the party; if you can't go physically try to find some pictures of it on the internet to look at and talk about.

Make a schedule showing what will happen using visuals, words or props and include going home in order to reassure your child that the party will have an end and afterwards they will come home.

If you can stay it may help, but it may make the situation worse. You will be the best to decide as you know your child. If you think it would not help, speak to the party organiser and explain that your child has ASD and may need some quiet time or to leave early.

Ask if there is a quiet area where your child can go to if they become anxious, overwhelmed or tired. Show your child where it is and explain that they can ask to sit there.

Stay close to the venue – if you think your child will find the situation difficult don't leave, REMAIN on the periphery.

Alternatively, return early after reassuring your child by telling them that you will only be gone for a short while (a slightly shorter time than you anticipate they can tolerate).

Make sure you can be reached and don't go too far away just in case your child becomes distressed.

Leave the party before your child becomes anxious or distressed then they will retain a positive image of the whole event which can be built on the next time.

Chapter Fifteen
ROUTES –
THE BENEFIT OF VARIATION

We all tend to use familiar routes but as children with ASD pay great attention to detail they can be quite adamant about which way you go and how you travel, which can cause considerable problems.

Children can become quite fixated on which way you walk or drive to a particular venue and become insistent that it is precisely the same route each time. On the face of it this doesn't sound like too much of a problem although it can be, for example:

- If you walk the same route every day, what happens if the pavement is being dug up and you need to cross the road?
- If you drive every day, what happens if the car doesn't work one day or needs to go in for a service?

Maybe you aren't able to take your child to school for some reason and you need to drop them off for another parent to take them – if they have never done this before it may make them extremely anxious.

Your child may anticipate where you are going from

the route you take which can also cause them anxiety; for example, if you drive past the park and have stopped there to play once they may not understand that you are not going to stop there every day.

Not all children with ASD will have this extreme desire for sameness which can affect the route you take but in case it develops it is important to be aware of following the same route and plan changes into your trips regularly in order to avoid any future problems.

Sami

Sami would go home from school by car but often became very anxious as he left school and would cry and scream once he was in the car until he got home. This behaviour continued for some time and became more and more difficult for his mother. When his mother told me about this behaviour I suggested to her that she use 'now and next' pictures to help Sami understand that he was going home.

Now	Next
Car	Dog

I asked his mother what he liked to do when he got home and she told me he would run straight to their new dog which he loved to cuddle and stroke. I made his mother two cards – one with a picture of her car and the other with a picture of his dog. It worked well – Sami stopped the crying and screaming and willingly got in the car to go home. He would hold the picture of the car and his dog and seemed to at last understand that he was going home.

Chapter Sixteen
STARTING SCHOOL – ROUTINES, LUNCH AND PLAYTIMES

What are the problems and how to minimise anxieties and difficulties.

1. The building, an unfamiliar location

It is important to ask the school if your child can make a few visits before they are due to start attending, starting with a short visit for maybe half an hour and gradually increasing this to a couple of hours.

Ask the school if they can make you a book of pictures about the school, including teachers, toilets, dining halls, assembly or PE halls, outside areas and the entrance they will use when they start. Look at the book regularly in the holidays to familiarise your child with what to expect.

If it is at all possible, walk or drive past the school during the holidays and point it out to your child, saying 'school'.

Ask if your child can be in the first group of children to start.

There will be more opportunity to explore the classroom in a calmer more spacious environment. It will allow your child to become familiar with a few children before the classroom becomes more crowded.

The noise level will be lower.

If there is a quiet area within the classroom ask if your child can be taken there if they are overwhelmed and anxious. If this is possible, take them there yourself; ask if they could have access to a favourite toy or sensory box for exploration to help them feel calmer.

Ask if your child could start each day with a routine. You may well find that the teacher has a daily routine already but your child may benefit from an additional one. For example, being dropped off to their 'quiet space' (mentioned above) or being allowed to play with construction, the home corner or cars as a first activity each day, whichever is their preferred activity.

They may benefit from sitting at the same table or with the same activity each morning. However, beware of your child's liking for sameness causing undue stress and don't use this constantly during the day. Ask the teacher if they can vary the activity slightly or change the table used, e.g. move the chair, put different activities on the set table or add another dimension to the activity – maybe a different helper.

2. Fire alarms

The first fire alarm practice often causes a lot of anxiety for a child with ASD. It may be beneficial to ask the teacher if they can make a recording of the fire alarm and gradually expose your child to the noise for brief periods, e.g. seconds to start with, very gradually increasing (perhaps they could control the on and off switch).

Ask the teacher if they can follow the route regularly in order that your child doesn't become too upset and anxious if the alarm goes off. Suggest that your child has some support to make a book about fire procedures and practices that they can look at to familiarise themselves with the process.

3. Snack time

Nursery and reception classes generally have snack time every day. In some nurseries children can take their snack at any time, whilst in others it is a social event where they all sit together either at the table or on the carpet. At this time they will have the opportunity to eat fruit and have a drink. Many children with ASD are fussy eaters so if this applies to your child ask the teacher what snack and drink will be available and explain that your child only likes banana, for example. Alternatively, ask them if you can take your child's snack in each day so that they can eat their own food but still join in socially.

I have known parents bring in dried mango, cucumber or dry cereal, and teachers are usually only too pleased to offer what has been sent in and see children enjoying these opportunities to eat, drink, and hopefully communicate with their peers.

4. Lunchtime

The dinner hall is often an extremely difficult environment, full of smells, noise and many moving bodies, just to name a few problems.

Some schools will let your child eat in a quieter area which may reduce anxiety.

Give your child a familiar lunch; a packed lunch may be better to begin with if they are a fussy eater, but introduce them to using a packed lunch at home first so that they have the chance to become familiar with opening containers and eating from boxes and bags, etc.

School dinners are great for the less fussy eaters but check the menu before you decide – the school will generally have weekly menus printed that they can give you on request.

To assist with new tastes or dishes you could try less familiar meals at home first.

Your child may benefit from a schedule to follow, for example, a list of items to help them understand the routine as well as to help them decide what order they will eat in as the choice can be overwhelming.

Examples of lunchtime schedules:

Drink	Sandwich	Jelly	Cake

Cucumber	Drink	Apple	Jelly

Remember, it doesn't have to be a sandwich as some children like cold pizza or plain pasta – give them something they enjoy.

5. Social opportunities at playtime

Whilst we may all want our children to socialise and make friends, they may like some time to play alone, with a familiar adult or just one familiar peer or sibling to help reduce anxiety levels. However, this is also a great opportunity for exercise, making friends and learning to take turns and negotiating with peers, which should not be overlooked.

Some children like to walk around with dinner staff in the playground but this may reduce opportunities to make friends and play with their peers. It is extremely helpful if the staff help your child ask to join in games and activities with their peers, for example, racing and chasing. I have seen many children with ASD giggling and looking for someone to chase them. By their peers and adults regularly joining them in this game, children have learnt how to chase back and really enjoyed the experience. It is, however, difficult for them to make friends if they hold an adult's hand and walk around the playground for the whole period glued to an adult's side.

Your child may benefit from having a buddy allocated or choosing their own friend each day; even if they only play together for a few minutes, this helps them become less anxious of other children and equally encourages their peers to become less anxious and more understanding of their behaviour and needs.

Some schools have a nurture group – a place where a small group of children who find it difficult to cope with the noise and busy environment of the playground (for various reasons) can spend time, and where there are games and activities available.

6. Taking your child home for lunch

Some parents prefer to take their children home for lunch because of the difficulties of eating lunch; however, this results in them missing the lunch playtime and the opportunities that this provides for them to play with peers and learn related social skills.

Think carefully about making a decision to take your children home at lunchtime. There are other options if your child refuses to eat or drink at lunchtime. Ask the school if your child would be able to have a snack later during the afternoon if they haven't eaten or drunk at lunchtime.

Chapter Seventeen
SELF-DIRECTION OR ACCEPTING ADULT DIRECTION

Some children are extremely self-directed and resist adult direction often because they don't understand the expectations and they become anxious. They may fear the activity will never finish and need some assurance; using a visual structure to show them the order of their day often helps. It is the equivalent of a diary; it can be in words if your child understands words, pictures or symbols if they don't. If they don't understand that pictures represent objects or activities, you can use objects.

To introduce visual structure initially just use two items, e.g. 'now and next' then gradually build up to the sequence of events but don't rush – keep it manageable for your child and yourself. Personally, I would also keep a 'now and next' in my bag whenever possible as this may also help to calm your child when away from home. If they know they are going home or having a favourite treat after they have completed an activity or essential trip it may help them feel less anxious. You can use photos and symbols –

in colour or black and white – or objects, whichever works best for your child.

Some examples of visual structure:

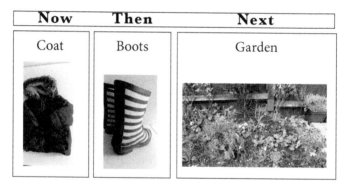

If your child does not understand that photos or pictures represent real objects, show them the real things in the order in which you want them to be done.

Peter

Peter did not understand what was happening when his mother brought him to school. He didn't understand that pictures represented objects. He consequently became even more upset when he went outside with his coat on – he thought his mother was coming to take him home and he would stand at the fence staring at the school gate. We asked his mother to give him a scarf which he should only wear when she brought him to school or collected him at home time. When Peter arrived each morning we would take the scarf and put it on top of the cupboard where he could see it but not pull it down. He gradually learnt that when his scarf was put on the cupboard he would stay at school and when it came down it was home time. We extended this to familiarise Peter with the routine of the day – Peter needed a shelf rather than a picture timetable. It would have a cup to represent a drink, toilet paper to represent a visit to the toilet and then, dependent upon what activities were being offered, for example, a Lego piece represented a Lego activity, a paintbrush represented painting and a rolling pin represented a Play-Doh activity. This helped Peter to understand what he would be doing and helped reduce his anxiety.

After some weeks we also introduced a picture for each activity as well as the object and helped Peter to match the two together. It took some time but now Peter understands that pictures represent objects and he is able to use a visual (picture) timetable. He now has a much better understanding of the routine at school. He no longer needs his scarf to remind him its home time, instead we had a picture of his mother on his timetable at the end of the day.

Chapter Eighteen
SENSORY ISSUES –
HYPO AND HYPER
SENSITIVITIES

It is important to remember that a child with ASD may be affected by (hypo) under and (hyper) over sensitivities in any combination: auditory (hearing), olfactory (smell), touch, visual.

An appreciation of the impact is really important if we are to try to understand children with ASD's difficulties and how these impact on their everyday lives.

You and I may be able to filter out the noise of a clock ticking, the hum of the refrigerator and the babble of people speaking in another room – imagine if we couldn't.

We can usually filter out the smell of garlic, the cleaner on the worktops and the food in the fridge – imagine if we couldn't.

We can probably ignore the flicker of a strip light, the flashing LED on the carbon dioxide monitor and light sensors in our gardens – imagine if they were confusing our eyes and constantly interfering with our sight.

Some of us don't like the feel of chalk on a blackboard or having sticky fingers, walking on lumpy floors or wearing new shoes that feel different, but we can tolerate these things. Imagine if we couldn't think about anything else; it would be like having an allergy and constantly exposing yourself to it.

I cannot imagine or describe all of the sensory issues or combinations of these that can occur as they differ in every individual child.

Corey

Corey had a table to work at next to the heater when I first worked with him. In the winter his behaviour was significantly worse than in the summer. He was extremely anxious and would push furniture over with his feet, sometimes pinching his support staff and kicking them.

After talking with parents and other staff we discovered he was generally quite a hot child and rarely needed a coat.

When we moved his table away from the radiator his behaviour was much improved.

Nelson

Nelson had an accident and wet his trousers and he was changed into some second-hand spare jeans we had for such events. He then started to wet himself every day, sometimes several times. His parents could shed no light on this change in his behaviour and were as concerned as the school. We noticed that when Nelson wet himself, he wanted to get the spare clothes out of the cupboard himself and we thought it may be the washing powder smell that he liked. We suggested to his mum that she use the same powder; she did but the wetting continued. After two or three weeks we were still unable to find the cause of the wetting. One day, Nelson refused to put on clean trousers and he threw them across the room. We presented them to him again and repeated 'trousers on'. He took them, found an empty box put them in, shut the flaps down and pushed them under a chair. We began to think it was something about the trousers so we brought a selection of styles and materials. When he saw a pair of jeans amongst them he smiled and put them on; a bit of detective work revealed that the first time he had wet himself he was given jeans and someone had said to him "O Nelson, you do look smart". The solution was so simple; we asked his mother to buy him some jeans to wear to school (any make that was not expensive) – she did and he didn't wet himself again.

Chapter Nineteen
SENSORY ISSUES –
DEFINITIONS

Auditory – hearing

Under-sensitive – this could be to a specific pitch rather than difficulty hearing and it may affect the hearing of some sounds and not others. Your child may like to put their hands over their ears and then take them off repeatedly, to make the sounds more interesting (people often think that children are trying not to listen which is not always the case).

Over-sensitive – this is a dislike of crowded noisy places, fire alarms, some pitches and volume. Children with over-sensitive hearing may hear things happening next door or outside in the street and they may find it hard to concentrate as they could be hearing sounds from the fridge, electric strip lights, washing machines and pipes which they cannot filter out.

Visual – sight

Under-sensitive – your child may enjoy flicking his hands in front of his eyes to make things appear more interesting, similar to a black and white strip film; your child may enjoy staring at bright lights from close proximity or enjoy turning lights on and off.

Over-sensitive – your child may have a dislike of bright lights, sometimes sunlight, bright colours and busy patterns. Children may find dark glasses help them to feel more comfortable.

Taste

Under-sensitive – your child may like strong flavours and enjoy eating non-foods which appeal to their sense of smell.

Over-sensitive – your child may have a dislike of strong flavours, they may be a fussy eater and prefer bland food or they may only eat certain textures, for example, crunchy or smooth foods.

Touch

Under-sensitive – your child may not know when they are hurt or ill; these children could injure themselves and show no awareness of discomfort. They could touch extremely hot or cold objects and show no reaction. Children who are under-sensitive to touch may prefer firm pressure when they are cuddled, firm massage and enjoy the feel of weighted blankets around them.

Over-sensitive – these children may prefer a very light touch and find hugs and squeezes painful. They may not like to touch certain substances, for example, paint, glue or sand and sandpaper. This may impact on their willingness to wear clothes made from certain fabrics.

Vestibular – sense of balance and gravity on our bodies

These children may like to be upside down or to lay on the floor looking at objects from unusual angles.

I have worked with a number of children with ASD who had no idea of where or how to sit on the carpet. When they were given a carpet square to sit on, placed close to the other children and near to the teacher, they quickly learnt to keep their bodies on the square and to walk to it when they came in. Alternatively, I have made rule books with pictures of how to sit appropriately (photos of the child themselves and/or their peers sitting appropriately, e.g. listening, hands in their lap to avoid touching the other children, trying to sit in one place). I looked at these each day with the children, sometimes using them as a reminder while the child was in situ on the carpet if they were acting inappropriately, and generally these produced some good results.

Jerry

Jerry liked to spend as much time as possible upside down, tumbling over furniture as often as he could. I would estimate that he spent 60% of his time upside down. He responded well to a weighted scarf placed around his neck to help him have a sense of grounding. His difficulty related to proprioception – a sense of where his body was in relation to the surroundings as indicated by his muscles and limbs.

Samuel

Samuel loved hair so much he just couldn't resist playing with the long hair of the girls in his class during carpet time or the tassels on his teacher's boots. His response to "no" was short-lived and needed to be repeated constantly. To provide support for the teacher we also taught the children to say "no" when Samuel reached to touch them or became too near for their comfort. Much to our surprise, but relief, he responded more consistently to them than to his teacher. His hair-stroking and tassel-touching ceased.

Christopher

Christopher liked to touch the staff's hair; he responded well to being allowed to comb a doll's hair rather than the children's or the teacher's hair.

Mary

Mary liked to sit with the other children on the carpet but had no awareness of facing the teacher when the teacher was talking. She would face any direction quite randomly, but with the help of a cushion with a pattern on it Mary learnt to face the right way in order that her gaze was directed in the correct direction and she consequently became more aware of the teacher leading the lesson.

Chapter Twenty
SHARING –
A SKILL FOR LIFE

This is an important skill not only for school but for life. Your child may find it difficult to share with you or their siblings at home. The answer isn't to avoid sharing – in fact this may make the situation escalate and will impact on their school life as well as at home. If they can't share with you how will they share and play with their peers?

Set out below are some ideas for developing sharing at home.

If your child likes to line things up or collect all of any similar toys (possibly from their siblings or friends):

- Walk past and touch something in the line. Do this several times maybe over several days if need be until they can tolerate this.
- Pick up an item, raise it slightly from the line and replace it quickly; repeat this until your child is able to accept this interference with their play.
- Pick up an item, bringing it up to your eye level, look at it and replace it; repeat this until your child is able to tolerate this.
- Pick up an item, look at it and put it in another position,

but allow your child to replace it wherever they like.
- Make a habit of using this strategy to alleviate their anxiety about others touching their lines or toys.

Using Intensive Interaction (Nind and Hewitt, 2001)

This intervention involves copying your child's movements or sounds, always following their lead, and stopping if they indicate that they aren't happy or they move away.

If your child is lining up toys make your own line or game either with the same objects or different ones. If your child reaches for one of yours, reach for one of theirs; if they take one of yours, take one of theirs. Repeat and copy their actions.

If you have pairs of some items, allow your child to select one; follow their lead, for example, if they shake a tambourine, you shake a tambourine, etc.

You can use this strategy in all contexts and it's an important concept for your child to learn, even with their favourite food; for example, if they have a bag of crisps, always have one yourself or give one to their siblings – it will help them be more tolerant of others and may help reduce or avoid some anxieties and related tantrums.

These ideas will help encourage your child to tolerate your interference and learn to share as they become reassured that their items will not be taken away forever. They may even develop into short games.

I have used intensive interaction many times in my work and I also carried out a study of using it with children at home – many of these copying sessions often extended into a type of play for in excess of twenty minutes.

Chapter Twenty-One
SHOES –
WEARING NEW SHOES

Children's feet are soft and pliable so the right fit is exceedingly important; however, for a child with ASD who doesn't understand why he or she has to wear new shoes (which generally aren't comfortable for anyone straight away), it can be a major difficulty.

Many children with ASD prefer to walk barefoot and many walk on their toes. This can be due to a variety of reasons which should be discussed with an occupational therapist as it is possible it could cause a long-term problem in later life. Some children with ASD are prescribed orthotic inner soles, others exercise, but it is important to get specialist advice.

We all have our preference for colour and style; we probably know our shoe size and which styles suit us best, taking into account comfort and fashion. Children with ASD have their preferences too, although they aren't always able to verbalise or communicate to us what they are. We may be able to identify that part of a shoe is stiff and uncomfortable whereas a child with ASD may not, due to over or under sensitivities. This in turn can result in children getting sore feet and refusing to put the shoes on, continuing to wear them until it becomes obvious to parents as they help them dress, or their child adopts an unusual walk to compensate.

Below are some ideas to help children accept and wear new shoes in the general context of growing feet and worn-out shoes. It is inevitable that children will need new shoes so we need a strategy to help them accept the change.

Some parents will buy the same shoes in increasing sizes which works well until they go out of stock or fashion. Some parents choose shoes that their children cannot take off, e.g. laces; this may be a potential solution but could result in your child refusing to walk anywhere, becoming anxious and having a tantrum. If you give in and revert to the old shoes you will find yourself back at the start with the new shoes, as your child may have learnt that if they have a tantrum the shoes come off – not the result you are hoping for. Your child may benefit from inner soles with patterns on and these can be transferred to the new shoes and replaced at a later date. Your child may like to choose the shoes with you; you could look at catalogues together or the internet and see which ones they seem to like. This will also help minimise the time that you have to spend in the shop if this is an issue.

If possible, keep the old shoes (if they aren't too small) and encourage your child to wear the new ones for a short time. Take the new shoes off whilst your child is happy, not whilst they are screaming or having a tantrum, as this will also give them the wrong message (as above). Allow them to take off the new shoes and wear the old ones for a while, gradually increasing the time that they spend in the new shoes.

Distraction sometimes works – if you can get your child to put the new shoes on give them a treat/reward to encourage them to want to wear them.

If they are close to a brother, sister or friends, see if they can go to the shop with you – often "wow, they look nice" is well received, especially if it comes from their special friends as well as their parents. Alternatively, take two members of the family to the shoe shop to get new shoes at the same time as this may also help.

Chapter Twenty-Two
SHOPPING –
A NECESSITY

Shopping is a necessity; although we can now use the Internet for many items, it is unlikely that we can avoid shopping altogether. Shops present a variety of sensory experiences that may be difficult for your child to tolerate:

- Bright lights
- Smells of various merchandise
- Crowds in aisles and queues at tills, people pushing trolleys in a variety of directions
- Temptations on offer, items that your child is not allowed to touch or have, although they can sometimes (this may cause a lot of confusion and anxiety)

Advance planning may help your child to cope and tolerate the experience.

Talk about where you are going and what you might buy – you can use objects from your cupboards and fridge to help your child understand and become familiar with the names of items if they have problems understanding or recalling what things are called.

Tullamore Library

Issue Summary

Patron:
Id: 2001**********
Date: 27/08/2020 11:51

Loaned today

Item: 30013004883515
Title: Autism supporting difficulties :
 handbook of ideas to reduce
 anxiety in everyday situations.
Due back: 17-09-20

Item: 30013005577264
Title: Sound by sound. Part 1,
 Discovering the sounds / Ann
 Sullivan.
Due back: 17-09-20

Thank you for using self service

Give your child a label from something that you want to buy which they can take with them and match to the item in the supermarket.

Make a shopping list by writing, sticking labels on paper, drawing or listing items by name/photo or picture on an iPad.

It may be easier for your child if the trip is not too long and followed by a preferred activity, for example, a trip to the park or five minutes of playing with a favourite toy or activity.

Keep to your plan and leave the shop before your child becomes anxious, even if it means leaving the shopping behind because of a queue. It is always better to finish on a positive note and whilst your child is happy.

Some parents like to buy their child something as a reward for going to the shops, but it may be better to do this sometimes rather than always; it can prove expensive or you may not always be able to find something that they want.

If you buy your child the same item every week, what will happen if it is out of stock? If, however, you do decide to buy your child the same reward every week, remember to explain this to anyone else who takes them shopping as without this reward your child may have a tantrum.

It may help your child if you vary the route that you take around the shops or supermarket. Your child may become distressed if you walk around one way several times and then try to vary your route. It may only take a few weeks before a route becomes ingrained, and thereby difficult to change.

Chapter Twenty-Three
SPATIAL AWARENESS – UNDERSTANDING THEIR OWN SPACE

Some children with ASD find it hard to negotiate space for a variety of reasons. Some have difficulty identifying where their bodies finish and where space begins and others find it hard to determine depth, for example, on stairs.

It may be that your child finds it difficult to sit in a small space due to a lack of spatial awareness. They may benefit from a carpet square or circle, a particular cushion, a piece of fabric, or to sit in a regular position, as otherwise they may sit on or walk on their brothers, sisters or peers at school unintentionally.

Coming down stairs may be especially difficult – imagine if you couldn't judge the depth of the stair and weren't sure how far down to put your foot. I am sure most of us have at some time missed the last stair and experienced that scary sensation of falling. It may help your child if the edge of the stairs are marked with chalk, sticky tape or paint, depending on the covering, if they find this difficult to judge and negotiate.

If your child seems to find it difficult to negotiate space they may also benefit from clearly defined areas, e.g. using a different floor covering or as above – chalk or sticky tape to mark areas where they can or can't go.

Spatial awareness also has quite an impact on socialising. Most of us don't like people invading our personal space but for a child or young adult with ASD this may be quite difficult to determine. I have seen many children and young adults with ASD looking into someone's face from a few inches to gain their attention. If your child does this, it may be useful to show them how to gauge an appropriate distance. Perhaps you could suggest they stretch out an arm and if they can touch the person they are too close. You can simultaneously teach them that it is different for family members and that you can be a little closer to them.

Scott

Scott liked to crowd surf on the carpet at school. When the children were on the carpet he would simply throw himself on top of them and loved to hear them squealing as a result. Scott would also walk through them if he needed to get up and come to the front. We solved this by simply giving him a carpet square so he knew where to sit and maintaining a clear route to the teacher between the other children.

Nicholas

Nicholas found it difficult to stay upright. He liked to constantly tumble over his mother's shoulder. An occupational therapist solved this problem by suggesting he wore a weight around his neck (no expense incurred as his mother used a pair of tights filled with lentils). There are also manufactured weighted jackets, blankets, etc. that you can purchase to solve this but lentils are much cheaper!

Chapter Twenty-Four
SPECIAL INTERESTS –
HOBBIES

We all have special interests and for most people they form the basis of our hobbies, for example, sports, gardening, music or collecting items from a particular category.

For children with ASD, special interests are far more important and may take up an increasing amount of their day. If the time spent indulging in special interests is left unchecked it can cause difficulty in relation to your child's ability to focus in other areas.

Special interests have a purpose. They are relaxing – if a child is extremely focused on their interest, it can help shut out causes of anxiety around them such as unfamiliar environments. However, there are some special interests that are socially unacceptable in our society, for example, playing with saliva. We may be able to help our children replace this with something more acceptable, for example, PVA glue or gloop. Alternatively, we can try to teach our children that although they can play with saliva at certain times, at others or in other contexts they should use an alternative. You can help your child to do this by keeping a watchful eye and giving them opportunities to play with PVA, or whatever the substitute item is, at regular intervals throughout their day, using it as a reward or to help them self-soothe when we can see that they are becoming anxious.

Children with ASD need to be allowed to indulge in their special interests but not for indefinite periods. They can be a useful tool for learning, either as a reward or a resource.

I worked with a little girl who liked toothbrushes. We learnt to count from one to three using toothbrushes, how to sort using different colours, and big and small using different sizes.

I have used toy cars and trains in the same way.

You could try using the interest as a reward, for example, if your child likes Lego, give them a brick to play with each time they complete a task you have asked them to, for example, 'now wash your hands, next brick'.

In some cases special interests may form the basis of a career or become a future hobby:

- Running – running or marathons
- Jumping – trampolining
- Collecting – stamps, car models, trains, books about a particular subject, cataloguing
- Lining up – can help with organisation and sorting

You may be able to help your child manage their interests or alter them slightly to make them more acceptable. This will help to ensure that the interests don't dominate their lives and they are able to learn new skills; however, they should all be given some time to indulge in their special interests in order to help them manage or reduce their anxiety and help them relax.

Chapter Twenty-Five
TAKING TURNS AND LINING UP OBJECTS – JOINING IN

Often we don't interfere with our children's play; after all, it does give us time to catch up on jobs, have a short break or simply sit down and rest for a few minutes. Watching our children enjoy reading, play with their favourite toys or indulge in their special interest, for example, lining up items, spinning, mouthing or exploring objects all have their place as long as it is not for an excessive amount of time. We all need a break and so do children with or without ASD.

I agree that every child needs time to explore, make their own choice of play or have time for their special interest. However, for a child with ASD who has an overriding desire for sameness and routine, the more the play remains undisturbed the more of a ritual it becomes and the more difficult for the child to tolerate changes or someone else touching their play items.

Children with ASD are very strong-willed and if allowed to have their own way once will expect it every time. Even if we resist allowing them to do things, thirteen out of fourteen times the child will remember the time they got their own way and will keep on trying to gain it again by whatever means are effective, e.g. continual requests, screaming, hitting, throwing, etc.

As well as the need for sameness and routine, children with ASD have difficulty socialising and interacting, which we discussed earlier in the book.

Ideas of how to join in:

- Touch what your child is playing with; they will probably moan or push you away initially – this may be because they are worried that you will take the item and they will not get it back. Touch items your child is playing with just for a second initially, repeat this and extend the time until they are not at all upset by your actions. This part could take a few minutes, an hour or days or weeks. **DON'T MOVE ON TO THE NEXT STEP UNTIL YOUR CHILD IS ABLE TO ACCEPT YOU TOUCHING THEIR ITEM.**
- Pick the item up just above the floor or table for just a second and replace it in the same place; repeat as above until your child is able to tolerate this.
- Pick the item up, lift it slightly (a couple of centimetres) and put it back in the same place; repeat as above.
- Pick up the item, lift it up to eye level and put it straight back; repeat as above.
- Pick up the item, lift it up to eye level and put it back in a different place; repeat as above.

Try using Intensive Interaction (page 68) – copying your child's actions or using a like object of your own to mimic what they are doing.

Bill

Bill liked to line up small world characters. I used intensive interaction with him; I copied him by lining up my own equivalent toys. We continued to do this for several weeks, him lining up his toys and me lining up mine. Bill began to glance briefly at what I was doing and would sometimes pause to see if I would also pause. When I first started the intervention he would occasionally take one of 'my' toys and place it with his own, and in return I would try and take one of his (sometimes he didn't mind but sometimes I observed he was anxious so I would stop). Eventually, after some weeks, Bill would linger at his toy box when I arrived, looking at me and waiting for me to choose my toy to play with him, sharing a game rather than our initial parallel play.

Another simple prop for taking turns is a circle with a moveable pointer and photographs which indicate whose turn is next.

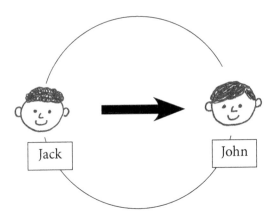

Jack

John

Chapter Twenty-Six
TEETH AND BRUSHING – THE IMPACT OF SENSORY ISSUES

Sensory issues have a significant impact on brushing teeth.

Co-ordination of brushing motion and placing toothbrush in correct position can be difficult. Visual appearance of brush and experience of putting non-foods in the mouth can be confusing

- Smell and taste of toothpaste – this may be overcome by using alternative flavours or powder toothpastes.
- Texture of brush – try hard or soft brushes as this will probably relate to sensory sensitivities whether they are hyper- or hypo-sensitive to touch.

If your child cannot tolerate hard or soft toothbrushes try using a rag rather than a toothbrush; once your child can tolerate this then slowly introduce the brush. Give your child the toothbrush to play with initially. If you use a flavour they like they may put it into their mouths themselves. If not, encourage them to let you put it into their mouth for a second or do it together hand on hand. Once they can accept the brush in their mouth, gradually extend the time, attempting one stroke on their teeth. You can build this up until either you or they themselves are able to brush their teeth effectively.

Taste/smell of toothpaste – try different flavours. Let your child smell different flavours as they will indicate which one they prefer. Observe their behaviour as they may move their nose or mouth towards the preferred flavour or move away from the one that they don't like.

Co-ordination of brushing motion – give them a mirror and practise side by side. They may benefit from having a short toothbrush to help stop them pushing it too far into their mouth or throat.

You can shorten a toothbrush by filing off the handle if this helps.

Visual appearance of toothbrush or toothpaste – use their favourite colour for both or take them to the shop to choose. There are some toothbrushes available with cartoon characters on that also flash for a minute whilst you brush. This may also entice your child to try and brush their teeth.

Alternatively, you could use 'now and next' using objects or pictures/photos.

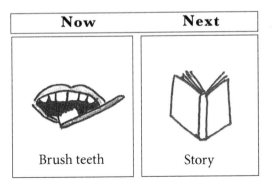

Now	**Next**
Brush teeth	Story

Chapter Twenty-Seven
TEXTURES –
SPECIAL INTERESTS AND
TOLERATING NEW TEXTURES

Some children with ASD find particular textures an irresistible special interest, for example:

- Playing with or smearing saliva. You could try and replace this with a more acceptable squeeze of PVA glue or bubble mixture on the table or in a saucer.
- Playing with or pulling hair. You could try and replace this with tassels made from wool or string of differing thicknesses, colours and textures.
- Tearing or flicking paper. You could try giving your child one book which they can flick or tear pages from, for example, giving them a catalogue, whenever time they attempt to tear or flick other pieces of paper.

Tolerating textures

If your child is anxious or reluctant when faced with particular textures you may need advice from an occupational therapist but the following suggestions may help.

If your child likes cars but not glue, use 'now and next', (e.g. now gluing, next cars,) supported by objects or pictures similar to those used on page 84 'Teeth and Brushing'.

Try extremely brief exposure to the texture, e.g. touching PVA glue then wiping finger immediately; repeat this regularly, very gradually increasing the time which you leave the glue on your child's finger or touching it twice before wiping.

If it's a fabric, put some over a favourite toy, show your child how you take it/lift it off, eventually encouraging your child to do it themselves.

Textures also affect eating, for example, children may only be able to tolerate:

- Slimy foods – spaghetti in sauce, custard
- Dry foods – anything in breadcrumbs, toast
- Wet foods – soups, milkshakes, drinks

Gradually introduce more foods of the same consistency, or replace part of the favoured food. Change the texture by grilling, boiling or liquidising. Always offer your child another choice or encourage them to try a small mouthful by offering a reward, for example, a biscuit or yoghurt dependent upon their preference (but don't give it until the new food is at least touched or explored in some way).

Cutlery can also provide different sensory experiences: wood is warm, stainless steel is cold, plastic can be either.

Similarly with plates or cups which are plastic, stainless steel or china. Try alternative tableware – it may help.

Proximity of food may affect a child's willingness to eat; some children with ASD will not eat food if it touches a different food and they may need their foods presented with space in between, on different plates or in separate bowls.

Solomon

Solomon liked to put his tongue in the cup to feel the water rather than to drink (which he would do from a bottle). By reducing the amount of drink in the cup, Solomon learnt that putting his tongue in the top of the cup didn't feel nearly as nice as the juice, and by tipping the cup back further to put his tongue in the liquid he had no option other than to drink as it trickled into his mouth.

Chapter Twenty-Eight
TOILETS AND HAND DRYERS – OVERCOMING FEARS

Toilets present a number of challenges.

They smell (cleaner or body odours) – olfactory. They often echo and are noisy – auditory. They have bright lights – visual. They are often quite small – spatial awareness. They contain water and unending rolls of paper – often irresistible to play with.

Hand dryers are loud and blow out hot air – For a child with ASD they appear to do this with no warning, indiscriminately and without moving, and in my experience are often the cause of children being too anxious to even enter the toilet area.

There are some things which we cannot remove from the toilets, especially when they are not in our own houses, for example, flickering strip lights, the smell and hand dryers. Even if our children use the toilet at home they may not use it outside of their home – in school or out shopping – so we have to accept that there may be some accidents at times.

Hand dryers

Sometimes there is a baby-changing facility, in which case you may be able to control and avoid using a hand dryer. If there is a switch by the hand dryer in the main toilet area explain to people that your child is frightened and ask them if they could wait until you exit to use the hand dryer – most people are quite understanding when children are involved.

Take a supply of tissues with you so that you can exit the toilet quickly and dry your child's hands outside of the area. You could take an antibacterial gel with you and avoid washing and drying if this causes distress.

Try taking earplugs, they may help some children if they would be happy to wear them and they may be more inclined to wear them if they are earplugs attached to a music-playing device, for example, an iPod.

If your child is, or becomes frightened of hand dryers, it may be very difficult to entice them back into the toilet area, and this can take a considerable amount of time to overcome.

Many children with special needs, especially ASD, find it extremely hard to overcome fears related to hand dryers but it is worth persevering as these are very difficult to avoid in public toilets and even in schools as so many places use this form of hand drying.

Michael

Michael took months to go into the school toilet due to his fear of the hand dryer. His mother told me that he had never used a toilet outside of the house (he was five years old). Initially it was all we could do to get Michael to stand outside the toilet; we managed to entice him in once or twice using a favourite toy, just for a few seconds. We would show him 'now and next' and gradually as the weeks went by we got him to go inside the doorway. After another few weeks we got Michael inside the cubicle and after becoming familiar with this we encouraged him to pull down his pull-ups and sit on the toilet. This went on for weeks but eventually Michael did start to use the toilet and he now uses toilets outside his house if he is out with his family.

Barry

Barry liked music and we decided to try to use it to entice him into the cubicle and to sit on the toilet. It worked well to begin with but Barry rarely used the toilet to urinate; perhaps he thought it was a seat to listen to music on. I am not sure whether it eventually worked as unfortunately he moved to another school, but this may be worth trying with other children.

Sometimes children will respond well to 'now and next' – now toilet, next a preferred activity. If they are in the midst of playing they may not want to move away, in which case you could try taking the toy with them to the toilet and placing it on a shelf until they have finished.

Chapter Twenty-nine
TOILET TRAINING –
WHEN IS THE RIGHT TIME?

The right time for toilet training is generally when your child becomes aware of when they are wet – generally not before, although I do know of children who were trained by taking them regularly; eventually they urinated on the toilet and stayed clean, despite showing no awareness of when they were wet when the training started.

Children with ASD can learn to use the toilet independently if they are aware of when they are wet and sometimes even if they are not, although it may take a little longer and it will need a consistent approach from you and playgroup or school if your child attends one of these.

- Firstly, keep a log of when your child wets himself, including how long after they have had a drink they urinate.
- You will need a large supply of clean pants as they may have a lot of accidents to begin with.
- Decide whether you will use a potty or a toilet.
- If you are going to use the toilet your child may prefer a smaller seat fitted on top of the adults' seat as this will stop them from slipping into the pan.

- Your child may also feel more secure with a foot stool as it can be hard for them to sit still if their feet don't touch the ground and are unsupported; alternatively, an upside down bowl works equally well depending upon their height.

Set a date and some time when you have no other distractions and are able to stay at home to concentrate on the training.

If you do need to go and buy any of the above items take your child with you and choose them together so that they feel involved.

Help your child put on the new pants and try not to let them wear the pull-ups during the day, as this may give mixed messages.

Your knowledge from the record of when they usually need the toilet may be useful but even if this information does not indicate any pattern, you should take them to the toilet every thirty minutes and help them adjust their clothing and sit on the toilet.

You could try giving them a drink of cold water just before you take them as this often increases the need to urinate.

Turning on the taps may also stimulate the need to urinate if they aren't sure what to do.

Keep repeating trips to the toilet as above at half-hourly intervals and watch for signs that they want to go. These may include: touching themselves, pulling at their clothing, holding themselves or jiggling around. If you see any of these signs that you think may indicate they are ready to urinate, take them to the toilet straight away and get them to sit on the seat in anticipation.

Use enthusiastic praise, even if they don't urinate, just for sitting on the toilet.

Make sure they feel secure when sitting on the toilet; they may get scared if they fall in the pan or lose their footing.

Once you have started the training don't put them back in pull-ups in the day as they may not sense as easily that they are wet. They also reduce the sensation of being wet; they may walk around in wet pull-ups quite happily whereas in pants they will probably be more aware and consequently keen to use the toilet. It may also confuse them and give them mixed messages if you change between pull-ups and pants.

Children will need reminders to use the toilet for some time as they can become very engaged in their play and forget that they need to go, or be frightened to leave an item in case it isn't there when they get back.

In school we sometimes take what they are playing with to the toilet with them and say, "Now toilet, next toy", placing it out of reach but within sight on a windowsill until they have finished. This often acts to reassure them that they are not missing out on anything and will encourage them to stay and use the toilet by reducing their anxieties.

It is sometimes a good idea to continue using pull-ups at night until your child becomes dry. This can be a different routine for the night-time; it will be much harder for them to sense they need to urinate when they are asleep. They may become dry at night in their own time which is kinder than waking them at night to use the toilet, and also allows you to rest at night.

Paul

Paul was unaware of when he was wet or soiled; he wore nappies that were changed regularly throughout the school day. Although we generally didn't start to train children until they showed some awareness of when they were soiled, we agreed with Paul's mother that we would take him to the toilet every half an hour at school to see if we could begin to help him use the toilet. We started by encouraging him to sit on the toilet; we noticed that he liked to play with the hand dryer so this became the reward for sitting on the toilet. We would put on the taps to encourage Paul to urinate, although it didn't seem to have any effect. To our surprise, after about two weeks we noticed Paul's nappies were staying dryer and he actually started to urinate in the toilet. We continued using pull-ups for another week then asked his mother to give us pants for him to wear at school. Paul remained dry in the pants and began to regularly use the toilet; each time he urinated we let him play with the hand dryer. Paul became almost fully toilet trained; although he never asked to use the toilet he still relied on staff taking him every half an hour, which was indicated by a picture symbol on his visual timetable.

Chapter Thirty
TRANSPORT – AEROPLANES – FIRST FLIGHTS

Preparation

Look at books about aeroplanes. Watch programmes about aeroplanes. Look at aeroplanes in the sky

Go to an airport and watch the planes going up and down, point and say 'plane' (simple, clear and concise language). Initially watch from the viewing area as the noise will be muffled and the lower volume may be easier to tolerate.

Try viewing planes from the outside if your child is able to tolerate the noise from the viewing area inside (remember the effect of the increased noise as it may present a considerable challenge to their tolerance and anxiety; be prepared to repeat the visit to the viewing area if it does).

Look at books about planes, and continue to watch them in the sky. Repeat visits to the airport regularly in the weeks before you fly, if at all possible.

Take some favourite toys or activities on the plane. Many children can be distracted by their special interests, for example, iPads, small world characters, light spinners or their favourite foods.

Remember that pressure affects your ears; bring a drink for your child to sip or something they can suck to help reduce the effect of the pressure changes.

Make sure you do something or they have something really special when they get off at the destination as they will remember this and it may help on future plane trips.

Advise the airline that your child has ASD when you book flights. They are generally very helpful and may allow you to bypass queues or sit next to vacant seats if there are any.

If you think your child might become very anxious, speak to your doctor and ask their advice; they may suggest something to help your child remain calm.

It may be an enjoyable experience to collect things from your trip, e.g. magazine, plastic spoon or anything your child finds interesting. You could use this on an aeroplane in the future, to remind them of that previous trip.

Chapter Thirty-One
TRANSPORT –
TRAINS AND COACHES

Look at books and films of trains and coaches several times.

Try to identify the possible causes of anxiety for your child before you get on a train or coach – sensory issues or fear of the unknown.

1. Noise
2. Smells
3. Space and proximity of others
4. Motion
5. Unknown out-of-normal routine

1. Noise

Gradually attempt to desensitise your child or young adult by slow exposure to trains/ coaches, e.g. watch trains/coaches from the outside of the station several times. Once the young person is able to tolerate the sound, move slightly nearer, working towards standing on the platform/coach terminus. Repeat this trip to the platform/coach terminus several times until they are happy to sit or stand and are able to tolerate the sound of train/coaches.

Get onto a train/coach and travel one stop, get off and if your child is not at all anxious make the one-stop journey back. If all goes well repeat this but for two stops and come back, extending the trip at each attempt. Be cautious about doing more; you should always aim to finish whilst your child is happy.

Repeat the train/coach journey, extending the route gradually as your child becomes more confident.

If at any time your child becomes anxious, back-step one stage until their confidence is regained.

2. Smells

This can be tricky but children may respond to distraction, possibly a favourite treat.

Try using 'now and next', e.g. now train/coach, next preferred activity. Support this by using pictures or visual cues, e.g. train ticket and bag of crisps, but don't be tempted to give all of the crisps until the trip is completed.

3. Space and proximity to others

Experiment with your position on the train. It may be that your child prefers to face the window and doesn't like people too near, or they may prefer a particular carriage. Show your child a train or coach picture or book and point to places where they could sit then ask them to choose which they would prefer. Take the picture or book with you and sit in the corresponding seats/carriage.

Look at model trains/coaches, count the trucks or seats and choose a particular numbered carriage or seat to sit in; find the same numbered carriage/seat on the real train/coach and sit in the equivalent place.

Give a choice to your child – "do you want to sit here or here?" (Only give two choices to keep it simple, as otherwise the decision may be too difficult for your child and cause anxiety.)

4. Motion

Try different parts of the train or coach; try facing different directions and encourage your child to choose.

Take a favourite toy or snack as a distraction.

Make a contract, e.g. train/coach first, then park (or an outing to a favourite place).

5. Unknown out-of-normal routine

Look at pictures of trains/coaches, take photos of trains and make a time to look at trains on the TV or internet.

Some children with ASD love train and coach trips or learn to if you take a graduated approach.

Chapter Thirty-Two
YOU –
LOOKING AFTER YOURSELF
AND CHOOSING YOUR
BATTLES

None of us has an indefinite supply of energy or patience. It is equally important that you look after yourself as well as your child with ASD.

I have recommended a lot of strategies and spoken about the need for consistency if we are to make progress, however we all get tired and sometimes don't have the energy to stand our ground and not give in.

For your child's benefit and your own it may be beneficial to pick your battles; don't try to deal with more than one difficulty or anxiety at a time. If you are tired, don't enter into confrontation or try to tackle too much at once. Children with ASD have notoriously good memories and if you challenge them and give in they will remember and keep on testing the boundaries with the hope that you will give in again.

Make sure you take some time for yourself to relax and recoup your energies; none of us can be perfect parents twenty-four hours per day without a break. If respite care is available take advantage of it, if there is a group of parents of children with ASD near you, join – it may provide the support and friendships that help you to begin to understand that you are not alone.

FOOTNOTE – YOU ARE NOT ALONE

Avoiding anxiety is the best course of action rather than dealing with the result.

Anxieties may recur; they do for us so why shouldn't they for children with ASD?

I have no cures to suggest but many strategies and interventions that I have used and which I hope will be of help in everyday situations which may be difficult for children with ASD.

Most areas have a group of parents of children with ASD – go along and make your own network of support.

Alternatively, there may be other parents at your child's school whose children have ASD – ask the school to arrange a coffee morning for you and get to know each other. Making friends with other parents of children with ASD provides a network of support and ideas which you can share. More importantly, it makes you realise that you are not alone!

I hope that you have found this book useful and a resource you can recommend to your friends.

Remember

Always

Look after yourself first

Choose your battles

Be consistent

Rewards or 'now and next' often work

REFERENCES

Bogdashina O., Sensory Perceptual Issues in Autism and Asperger Syndrome (2003), Jessica Kingsley Publishers

Gray C. and White A. L., My Social Stories Book (2002), Jessica Kingsley Publishers

Frost, L. and Bondy, A., The Picture Exchange Communication System Training Manual (2002), Pyramid Education Products Inc.

Nind M. and Hewitt D, A Practical Guide to Intensive Interaction (2001), British Institute of Learning Difficulties

I Can Kids Ltd, I can wash my hair DVD (2010), I Can Kids Ltd

Lightning Source UK Ltd.
Milton Keynes UK
UKOW07f1021141216
289979UK00012B/39/P